Families

by
Gail Saunders-Smith

Pebble Books
an imprint of Capstone Press

Pebble Books

Pebble Books are published by Capstone Press
818 North Willow Street, Mankato, Minnesota 56001
http://www.capstone-press.com

Library of Congress Cataloging-in-Publication Data
Saunders-Smith, Gail.
  Families/by Gail Saunders-Smith.
  p.cm.
  Includes bibliographical references (p. 23) and index.
  Summary: Describes the relationships among
members of a family, including grandparents, aunts
and uncles, and cousins.
  ISBN 1-56065-493-7
  1. Family--Juvenile literature. [1. Family.] I. Title.

HQ744.S28 1997
306.85--dc21
                    97-12693
                      CIP
                      AC

Editorial Credits
Lois Wallentine, editor; James Franklin, design;
Michelle L. Norstad, photo research

Photo Credits
FPG/Dennie Cody, 4; Arthur Tilley, 6; Adam Smith, 8
International Stock/Bill Stanton, cover
Unicorn Stock/Karen Mullen, 10; Jeff Greenberg, 1, 14;
  Chromosohm/Sohm, 16; Gerry Schnieders, 18; Ed Harp, 20
Valan Photos/Professor R.C. Simpson, 12

Table of Contents

This grandfather is playing with his grandsons.

This grandmother is kissing
her granddaughter.

This uncle is playing
with his nephew.

This aunt is talking
with her niece.

This sister is holding
her sister.

This sister is helping
her brother.

These brothers are riding
a scooter.

These cousins are playing a game.

20

These brothers and
sisters and cousins are
having fun.

Words to Know

aunt—your mother's or father's sister

brother—your mother's or father's son

cousin—your aunt's or uncle's child

grandfather—your mother's or father's father

grandmother—your mother's or father's mother

nephew—what a boy is to an aunt or uncle

niece—what a girl is to an aunt or uncle

sister—your mother's or father's daughter

uncle—your mother's or father's brother

Read More

Leedy, Loreen. *Who's Who in My Family?* New York: Holiday House, 1995.

Rosenberg, Maxine B. *Brothers and Sisters.* New York: Clarion Books, 1991.

Hausherr, Rosmarie. *Celebrating Families.* New York: Scholastic Press, 1997.

Internet Sites

Aunt Annie's Crafts
http://www.auntannie.com

Famdays Home Page
http://www.famday.com/famday.htm

Welcome to Family Internet
http://www.familyinternet.com/index.html

Note to Parents and Teachers

This book illustrates and describes relationships among members within a family. The clear photographs support the beginning reader in making and maintaining the meaning of the text. The verb allows teachers to introduce the "ing" ending. Children may need assistance in using the Table of Contents, Words to Know, Read More, Internet Sites, and Index/Word List sections of the book.

Index/Word List

Word Count: 60
Early-Intervention Level: 5